BBC
DOCTOR WHO

PAPER DOLLS

ILLUSTRATIONS BY BEN MORRIS
TEXT BY SIMON GUERRIER
AND CHRISTEL DEE

HARPER
DESIGN

An Imprint of HarperCollins Publishers

Contents

Introduction 5

An introduction to cosplay . . 6

The First Doctor 11

The Second Doctor 13

The Third Doctor 15

The Fourth Doctor 17

The Fifth Doctor 19

The Sixth Doctor 21

The Seventh Doctor 23

The Eighth Doctor 25

The Ninth Doctor 27

The Tenth Doctor 29

The Eleventh Doctor 31

The Twelfth Doctor 33

Jo Grant 35

Sarah Jane Smith 37

Romana 39

Ace 41

Rose Tyler 43

Donna Noble 45

Martha Jones 47

River Song 49

Amy Pond 51

Rory Williams 53

Clara Oswald 55

Petronella Osgood 57

Missy 59

Bill Potts 61

Introduction

"I have questions, but number one is this: what in the name of sanity have you got on your head?"

"It's a fez. I wear a fez now. Fezes are cool."

River Song and the Eleventh Doctor, *The Big Bang* (2010)

This book celebrates the brilliant, outlandish and sometimes downright peculiar costumes seen in more than 50 years of *Doctor Who*. With 26 dolls – including all 12 Doctors and a range of companions and characters, from Rose and Donna to Missy and Bill – and over 50 different outfits to change them into, you'll be able to cut out and dress up characters and – if you're feeling adventurous – even design some costumes of your own! There are fun facts on each outfit, explaining how the costume designer came up with it or why it's important to the episode's story. And if you're feeling especially inspired, read on for some tips on how to make your own versions of these outfits to wear!

Each incarnation of the Doctor has his own distinctive look. The First Doctor dresses as an Edwardian gentleman. The Third Doctor is all frilly shirts and velvet jackets. To the Eleventh Doctor, bow ties are cool. Each Doctor might try on different new items of clothing – a brighter waistcoat, a different colour tie – but their overall look remains largely the same.

The Doctor's companions – and many of his enemies – also have distinct ways of dressing. Clothes can even reveal the character of the person wearing them – and how they might be changing.

For example, when Rose Tyler sports an eye-catching Union Flag T-shirt in *The Empty Child* (2005), it's a sign of her growing confidence as she travels with the Doctor. She's not alone: many companions' choice of clothes gets bolder the longer they spend in the TARDIS (and the more they get to explore its vast wardrobe).

Of course, in real life what the Doctor and his friends wear is down to decisions made by the costume designers on *Doctor Who*, usually in conversation with the actors.

"I would never have thought that choosing some clothes would be of such importance to so many people," said Twelfth Doctor actor Peter Capaldi in 2016. "At the end of the day, I have to wear what makes me feel like Doctor Who – that's my rule. If it doesn't make me feel like Doctor Who, I don't wear it."

Ben, Christel and Simon

An introduction to cosplay

by Christel Dee

If after all this super crafty paper doll-making, you feel inspired to recreate some of the costumes yourself in real life, I've offered a few tips to help put together your very own *Doctor Who* cosplay!

Cosplay, short for "costume play", started in Japan, and is essentially dressing up as a character from a TV show, film, video game, book or comic. In recent years, we've seen an explosion of fans celebrating their favourite fictional characters through cosplay.

Costumes can range from the very elaborate to the very simple. Whether it's sourcing components for your costume, altering and repurposing clothing you have already or reinterpreting designs to make your own weird mash-up, cosplay is a great way to be creative and have fun!

If you've never cosplayed before, it might seem a little daunting. You may worry you don't have the budget, the art skills or feel you don't resemble the character enough. Well, first and most importantly, anyone can cosplay, including YOU! It doesn't matter what you look like, cosplay is for everyone. I hardly look like Peter Capaldi's Twelfth Doctor (who is tall, male and double my age!) but I love his character and his costume, which is the main reason I enjoy cosplaying him.

Cosplay doesn't have to be difficult to make or expensive to put together. I've been cosplaying for 10 years and have worked on costumes for numerous *Doctor Who* characters in that time. I've always liked to challenge myself and to try to make costumes that look accurate without spending hundreds of dollars. You'll be surprised how much you can transform something you already own by adding a bit of paint or tape, or swapping a few buttons. I've found many suitable items for cosplay by searching thrift shops and rummage sales, too.

The people making *Doctor Who* don't have inexhaustible budgets either, so they make do and mend too. For example, David Tennant's suit as the Tenth Doctor was made out of lots of pairs of trousers, while Jon Pertwee wore his own grandfather's old cape to the press call announcing he'd be the Third Doctor – and that became a signature part of his look.

What follows are a few simple, low budget cosplay ideas to help get those creative juices flowing, based on the fantastic *Doctor Who* costumes in this book. So strap in, and get your tape and scissors at the ready! And remember, these are just suggestions to get you thinking, not instructions of what to do.

We know you can do way better!

Top tips

Beg, borrow (don't steal)

Before you buy anything, see what's in your wardrobe already. You'll be surprised by how much you can recycle and transform by adding a bit of fabric paint or duct tape, or swapping some buttons. Rummage through your closet and see what can be repurposed. An old school blazer can be made into the First Doctor's black jacket by covering the emblem with duct tape or black fabric, while adding a red ribbon to an old straw hat makes it perfect for dressing up as the Fifth Doctor. Don't forget to ask your friends and family to look through their wardrobes too. Although make sure you ask – no stealing please!

Thrift shops

Thrift shops, vintage stores and rummage sales are usually the first place I go to when looking for clothes for cosplay. They are especially great for the more old-fashioned items of clothing for Classic Series characters. You'll be surprised how much you can find – and very cheaply too! It's super fun to shop around – you could even make a day of it and bring some friends!

Use the internet

I've been able to find so many weird and unusual items of clothing and materials for my cosplay pieces online. The internet has made it so easy to find all the things you need without having to set foot out the door! The downside is you can't try things on first; however, lots of places will let you return things if they're not suitable. It can take some time to find what you're looking for but be patient! Try different key words and filters and if you can't find what you're looking for right away, keep checking back as there are new items going up for sale all the time.

Think laterally

Coming up with cheap alternatives for cosplay pieces sometimes requires you to think outside the box. This is essentially looking at an everyday item of clothing or material and thinking what else it could be used for. For example, a cheap pair of pyjama bottoms would do nicely for the Second Doctor's chequered trousers. A large piece of ribbon can stand in for the Sixth Doctor's cravat (cake ribbons can be a great option, as they often have a wider range of patterns). You could even attach some string to a black tablecloth or bedsheet and use it for the First Doctor's cape!

Reuse and recycle

If you have a complete cosplay already and plan on starting a new one, it's worth checking to see if anything can be reused for another character. There are lots of similarities between the Classic Doctors' costumes in that many of them have shirts, waistcoats, chequered or striped trousers, coats and the occasional hat. Try things on to see what works!

Get shopping

The outfits worn by many of the characters in the post-2005 show are very contemporary which makes it easy to put together a costume using clothes from the high street. It's possible to buy screen-accurate replicas, although they can be tricky to track down and sometimes pricy. However, similar styles can be found almost everywhere. Series 10 companion Bill Potts is bang on trend and the shops are currently full of vintage band T-shirts and jackets with funky badges. The key is to get out there and get shopping!

Hair

It's up to you if you want to use your own hair or a wig. For your own hair, you can leave it exactly as it is or style it with products, and even dye it if you're that daring! I love to wear wigs because you can style them and keep them that way, so it's a lot less fuss when it comes to wearing the costume again. If you go down this route, it's useful to get a polystyrene head and some pins to keep the wig still, as that makes it much easier to style and store without the wig getting flattened. The other reason I like wigs is because they can completely transform your cosplay if your normal hair looks very different. But it's entirely down to personal preference!

Accessories

You can buy a lot of accessories, such as scarves, sonic screwdrivers and hats, but for things with more specific designs, you may need to do some arts and crafts! Why not try making a Sixth Doctor cat badge out of modelling clay, or creating Bill's badges by using fabric pen to draw designs onto white fabric? The Fifth Doctor's celery stick is easy to make by wrapping some green tissue paper around a piece of card and gluing on some scrunched up bits to make the leaves (real celery is not advised – it will wilt!). You can create the Second Doctor's recorder by wrapping light and dark blue electrical tape around a plain recorder... The list goes on! Start making!

Feel free to reinterpret

You don't have to replicate everything exactly as it appears on screen – unless you want to. Feel free to experiment and mix and match a character's outfits, or even mix the outfits with that of another character. You could do a mash-up of all the Doctors (I've seen this a few times!) or switch the gender of a character: How about a female Tenth Doctor with a brown pinstriped skirt or dress? You could even cosplay an object such as the TARDIS simply by wearing a blue outfit with a little light on your head!

Team up with your friends

Cosplay, in my opinion, is even more fun when shared with others! Why not team up with your friends and/or family and make it a group project? You could go as your favourite TARDIS team or even characters from specific episodes; e.g. the Tenth Doctor, Donna, Mr Halpern and Ood Sigma from *Planet of the Ood* (2008), the Twelfth Doctor, Clara, Rigsy and Ashildr from *Face the Raven* (2015) or the Fourth Doctor, Sarah Jane, Sutekh and a mummy from *Pyramids of Mars* (1975). Sharing cosplay can sometimes be more time- and cost-effective as you can buy your materials in bulk and share the workload within the group. It's also especially good when it comes to specific skills. If you're not particularly crafty but you have a friend or relative who is, you ask them to help with stuff like sewing buttons and gluing. Plus, working with others is a great way to keep you motivated to complete that cosplay project!

Where to cosplay

Some of the best places to show off your cosplay and meet other cosplayers are conventions, local events and screenings. Do some research to find out if there are any near you. You could bring along a friend or family member but if you don't know anyone who'd like to go, don't worry. You'll definitely meet other cosplayers there – it's a great place to make new friends! You can cosplay in public too. Organising cosplay meet-ups and photoshoots are great ways of doing this. You could even take your cosplay to the park and have a picnic. These are just some ideas but really, you can cosplay anywhere, whenever you feel like it.

Strike a pose

Once you have your completed costume and are ready to take it on its first outing, it's worth having a few poses up your sleeve as it's likely people will ask for your picture! Spend some time in front of the mirror with some pictures of your chosen character and practise. It may take some time to get right but be patient. It'll be worth it as the photos come out great and you won't feel caught out on the day.

Have fun

Cosplay is about having fun and celebrating your favourite characters and heroes. There are no rules so whether you want to buy or make your cosplay, if you want to try it, go for it!

An Unearthly Child (1963): Costume designed by Maureen Heneghan
The Reign of Terror (1964): Costume designed by Daphne Dare
The Web Planet (1965): Costume designed by Daphne Dare

THE FIRST DOCTOR

Played by William Hartnell
1963–1966, 1972–1973

The Doctor's hat is called a karakul, after the type of sheep whose fur it's made from.

This is the first outfit we ever saw the Doctor wear on screen, in the episode *An Unearthly Child.*

The clothes help suggest that actor William Hartnell is older than his 55 years.

To help with a special effects shot in *The Web Planet,* in this story the Doctor wears a white karakul hat rather than his usual black.

In *The Reign of Terror,* the sash signifies the Doctor's official position as a Regional Officer of the Provinces.

The Doctor temporarily hands over his ring to the Parisian tailor in exchange for these clothes.

The Power of the Daleks (1966): Costume designed by Sandra Reid
The Underwater Menace (1967): Costume designed by Juanita Waterson
The Abominable Snowmen (1967): Costume designed by Martin Baugh

THE SECOND DOCTOR

Played by Patrick Troughton
1966–1969, 1972–1973, 1983, 1985

When the Doctor wants Zaroff to see him, it's easy to shrug off the disguise.

Disguise worn in *The Underwater Menace* so Professor Zaroff won't spot him in the marketplace of Atlantis

The Second Doctor's "cosmic hobo" look — first seen in *The Power of the Daleks* — was suggested by Sydney Newman, the BBC's Head of Drama and co-creator of *Doctor Who*.

The new Doctor doesn't change his clothes — they seem to have regenerated with him!

This fur coat from *The Abominable Snowmen* is "just the thing" for the chilly climate of Tibet.

The recorder was Troughton's idea, to appeal to younger viewers.

Worn by the Second Doctor in his first three stories

Wearing this coat, the Doctor is quickly accused of murder — it makes him look like the Yeti that did it!

The Second Doctor wears a similar coat in *The Five Doctors* (1983).

13

Day of the Daleks (1972): Costume designed by Mary Husband
The Green Death (1973): Costume designed by Barbara Kidd
The Time Warrior (1973–1974): Costume designed by James Acheson

THE THIRD DOCTOR

Played by Jon Pertwee
1970–1974, 1983

Bright, colourful costumes because, with the début of the Third Doctor, *Doctor Who* now made in colour

Red smoking jacket first worn in *Terror of the Autons* (1971)

Inverness cape is sleeveless, leaving the arms free for fighting Ogrons

Green smoking jacket first worn in *Carnival of Monsters* (1973)

Jacket sold at auction in 2009 for £8,400

The Doctor dresses like this to sneak into the headquarters of sinister company Global Chemicals.

In *The Green Death*, the Doctor also disguises himself as a milkman.

Robot (1974–1975): Costume designed by James Acheson

The Talons of Weng-Chiang (1977): Costume designed by John Bloomfield

The Leisure Hive (1980): Costume designed by June Hudson

THE FOURTH DOCTOR

Played by Tom Baker
1974–1981

The Doctor's costume echoes the classic illustrations of Holmes, in Inverness cape and deerstalker, by Sydney Paget for *The Strand Magazine*.

The Talons of Weng-Chiang is set in the late 19th century and one key influence is Arthur Conan Doyle's Sherlock Holmes stories.

James Acheson unconsciously drew on an 1892 poster by Henri de Toulouse-Lautrec showing cabaret singer Aristide Bruant in a striking cape, hat and scarf.

Acheson commissioned Begonia Pope to knit the Doctor's scarf — and misunderstanding his instructions, she used all the wool she was given!

Tom Baker and producer Barry Letts wanted the Fourth Doctor to be less elegant and more bohemian-looking than the Third Doctor.

In 1980, new producer John Nathan-Turner asked June Hudson to design a smarter costume for the Fourth Doctor.

Hudson kept the basic silhouette — the scarf, hat and big coat — but in lusher fabrics and all in maroon.

Four to Doomsday (1982): Costume designed by Colin Lavers
Black Orchid (1982): Costume designed by Rosalind Ebbutt
The Awakening (1984): Costume designed by Jackie Southern

THE FIFTH DOCTOR

Played by Peter Davison

1981–1984, 2007

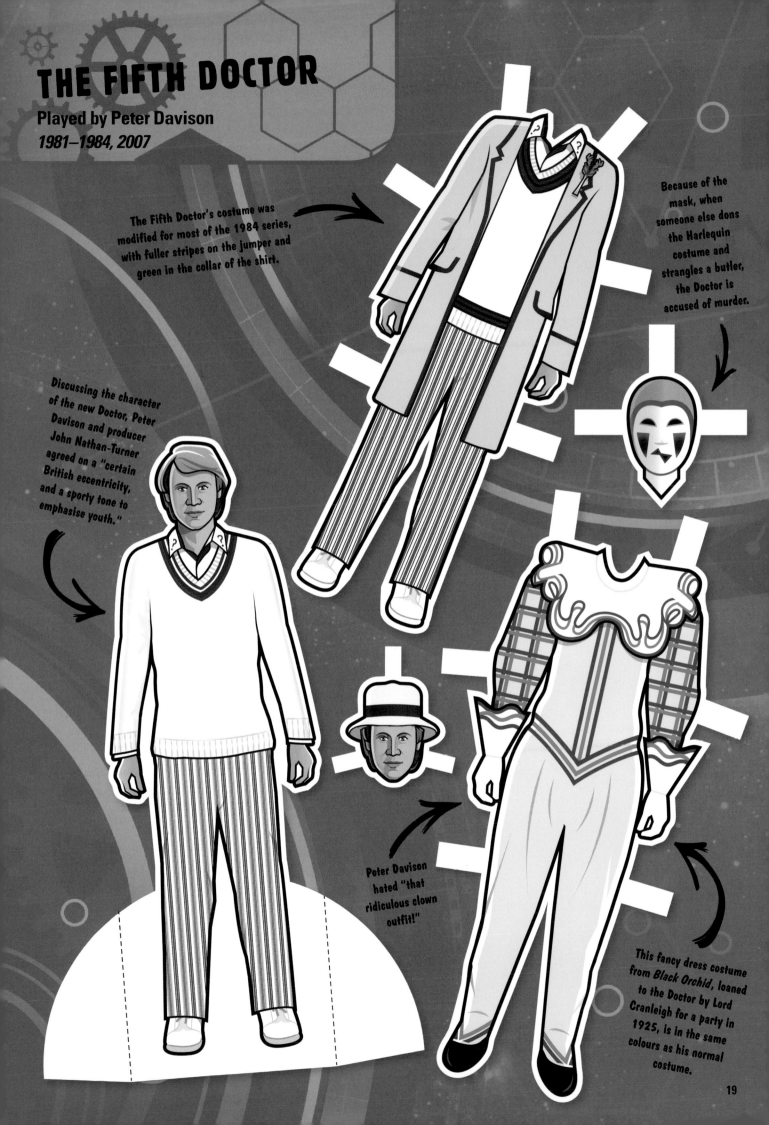

The Fifth Doctor's costume was modified for most of the 1984 series, with fuller stripes on the jumper and green in the collar of the shirt.

Because of the mask, when someone else dons the Harlequin costume and strangles a butler, the Doctor is accused of murder.

Discussing the character of the new Doctor, Peter Davison and producer John Nathan-Turner agreed on a "certain British eccentricity, and a sporty tone to emphasise youth."

Peter Davison hated "that ridiculous clown outfit!"

This fancy dress costume from *Black Orchid*, loaned to the Doctor by Lord Cranleigh for a party in 1925, is in the same colours as his normal costume.

The Two Doctors (1985): Costume designed by Jan Wright
Revelation of the Daleks (1985): Costume designed by Pat Godfrey
The Trial of a Time Lord parts 9 to 12 (1986): Costume designed by Andrew Rose

THE SIXTH DOCTOR

Played by Colin Baker
1984–1986

This costume contains no blue, which could cause problems for overlayed special effects.

The Trial of a Time Lord takes place in the Doctor's past, present and future. His clothes help us keep track of when events are occuring - the waistcoat, tie and cat badge are from the future part of the story.

The Sixth Doctor's costume, introduced in *The Twin Dilemma* (1984), was designed to be in "bad taste".

In *Revelation of the Daleks*, the Doctor is visiting a dying friend on the planet Necros, where blue is the colour of mourning.

Colin Baker wanted a suave costume of black velvet but this was too much like the Master!

Time and the Rani (1987): Costume designed by Ken Trew
The Curse of Fenric (1989): Costume designed by Ken Trew

THE SEVENTH DOCTOR

Played by Sylvester McCoy

1987–1989, 1996

Darker jacket to match the darker side of the Doctor being explored

Paisley scarf a nod to Sylvester McCoy's Scottish roots

The hat was based on the one Sylvester McCoy wore to his audition.

The idea was for the costume to look normal when seen from a distance, and eccentric only when seen up close.

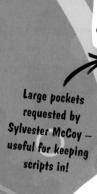

Large pockets requested by Sylvester McCoy — useful for keeping scripts in!

The duffle coat was originally just to keep Sylvester MoCoy warm on location — but he fell in love with it so it became part of the costume!

Doctor Who (1996): Costume designed by Jori Woodman
The Night of the Doctor (2013): Costume designed by Howard Burden

THE EIGHTH DOCTOR

Played by Paul McGann
1996, 2013

The Eighth Doctor "borrows" his outfit from a hospital in San Francisco on 31 December 1999.

This is really a costume for a fancy-dress party — he's dressed as gunfighter "Wild Bill" Hickok (1837–1876).

The Doctor has to "borrow" shoes from Grace Holloway's ex-boyfriend, Brian.

This new costume is based on the previous one, but designed to look more practical for (and battered by) years of adventuring.

Rose (2005): Costume designed by Lucinda Wright
Dalek (2005): Costume designed by Lucinda Wright
The Empty Child (2005): Costume designed by Lucinda Wright

Rose (2005): Costume designed by Lucinda Wright
Dalek (2005): Costume designed by Lucinda Wright
The Empty Child (2005): Costume designed by Lucinda Wright

THE NINTH DOCTOR

Played by Christopher Eccleston
2005

The production team on *Doctor Who* only ever had two versions of the Doctor's leather jacket. It was so precious it had its own security guard!

Stripped down, simple costume

Changing the Doctor's sweater but nothing else was a conscious choice. That way, he'd always be instantly recognisable.

"I didn't want the costume to be my performance," Christopher Eccleston said. "I wanted any flamboyance and colour to come out of my acting."

The Christmas Invasion (2005): Costume designed by Louise Page
Rise of the Cybermen (2006): Costume designed by Louise Page
Smith and Jones (2007): Costume designed by Louise Page

THE TENTH DOCTOR

Played by David Tennant
2006–2010

In *Gridlock*, the Doctor says his coat was given to him by singer Janis Joplin.

This look was inspired by chef Jamie Oliver's appearance on chat show *Parkinson* on 19 March 2005, wearing a pin-striped suit and trainers.

At the end of *Smith and Jones*, the Tenth Doctor proves to Martha Jones that he can travel in time by going back to the start of the episode and removing his tie in front of her.

David Tennant liked the fabric of a particular pair of trousers, so Page bought lots of pairs of those trousers and had his suit made from them.

Glasses let the Doctor see "void stuff" surrounding people who've travelled between parallel Earths

For the time travel scenes, the Doctor's in his brown suit, but for the rest of the episode (in between) he's in a new blue suit — making it easier for us to tell the difference!

Handmade Alain Mikli glasses — the production team only ever had one pair!

The Doctor first wears a tuxedo to pose as a waiter at a posh birthday party in *Rise of the Cybermen*.

The tux has the same shape as the brown suit, so he's instantly recognisable as the Doctor.

The Time of Angels (2010): Costume designed by Ray Holman
The Sarah Jane Adventures: Death of the Doctor (2010): Costume designed by Ray Holman
The Snowmen (2012): Costume designed by Howard Burden

THE ELEVENTH DOCTOR

Played by Matt Smith
2010–2013, 2014

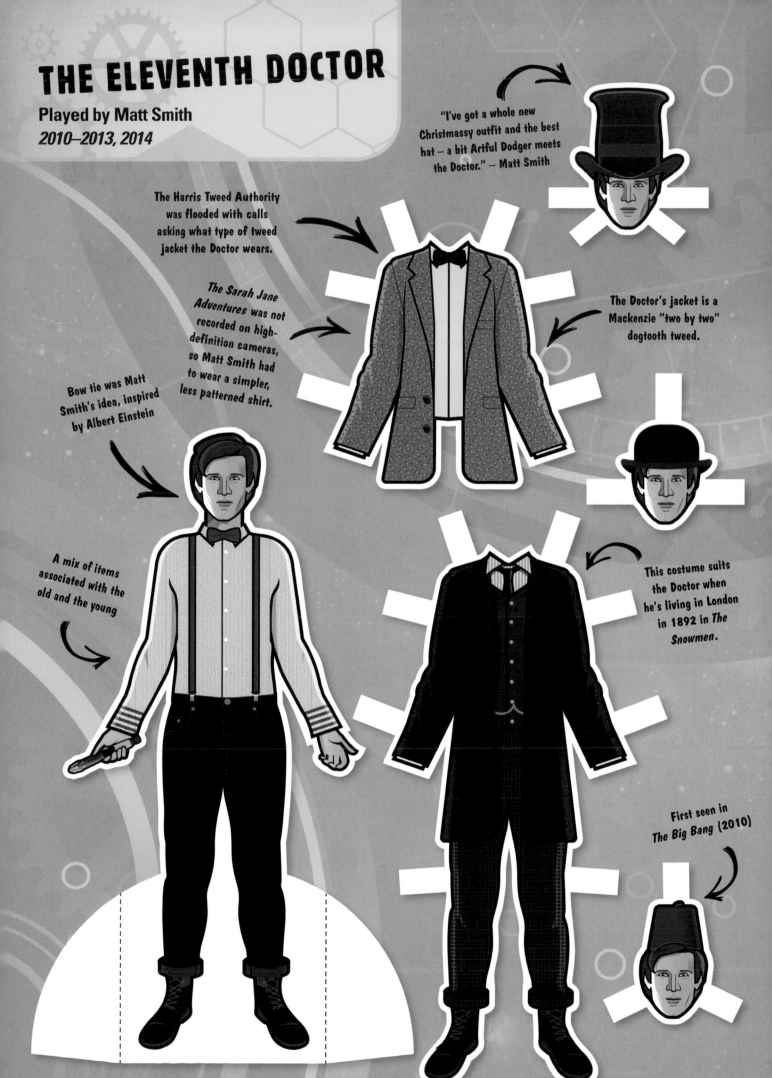

"I've got a whole new Christmassy outfit and the best hat – a bit Artful Dodger meets the Doctor." – Matt Smith

The Harris Tweed Authority was flooded with calls asking what type of tweed jacket the Doctor wears.

The Sarah Jane Adventures was not recorded on high-definition cameras, so Matt Smith had to wear a simpler, less patterned shirt.

The Doctor's jacket is a Mackenzie "two by two" dogtooth tweed.

Bow tie was Matt Smith's idea, inspired by Albert Einstein

A mix of items associated with the old and the young

This costume suits the Doctor when he's living in London in 1892 in *The Snowmen*.

First seen in *The Big Bang* (2010)

Deep Breath (2014): Costume designed by Howard Burden
The Magician's Apprentice (2015): Costume designed by Ray Holman
Face the Raven (2015): Costume designed by Ray Holman

THE TWELFTH DOCTOR

Played by Peter Capaldi

2013–2017

Sonic sunglasses — wearable technology that doesn't spoil the line of a jacket

"Simple, stark, and back to basics. No frills, no scarf, no messing, just 100% rebel Time Lord." — Peter Capaldi

Checked trousers from *The Magician's Apprentice* recall the Second Doctor's costume — a deliberate reference by Ray Holman

Day of the Daleks (1972): Costume designed by Mary Husband
The Curse of Peladon (1972): Costume designed by Barbara Lane
The Green Death (1973): Costume designed by Barbara Kidd

JOSEPHINE "JO" GRANT

Played by Katy Manning
1971–1973, 2010

Jo's outfit in *The Curse of Peladon* was perfect for passing as Earth royalty on the alien planet...

Jo's blue furry coat and thick polo-neck jumper from *The Green Death* were ideal for keeping warm in the Welsh quarries.

... or for a night out with UNIT's Captain Mike Yates.

"The little kiddies really got me. Older men found it quite pleasant to look at me. The mothers and girls didn't feel threatened and loved Jo's trendy clothes and rings." — Katy Manning

Not perfect for climbing a sheer cliff in a gale on the planet Peladon

Jo's high-heeled boots in *Day of the Daleks* were chosen for a practical reason: Katy Manning is 5' 1", but Third Doctor actor Jon Pertwee was 6'3".

Planet of the Spiders (1974): Costume designed by L Rowland-Warne
The Hand of Fear (1976): Costume designed by Barbara Lane
The Sarah Jane Adventures: Sky (2011): Costume designed by Stewart Meachem

SARAH JANE SMITH

Played by Elisabeth Sladen

1973–1976, 1981, 1983, 2006–2011

Elisabeth loved her costume. "We've found Sarah Jane an iconic look with the jacket and the boots," she said in 2010.

This stylish outfit was from fashionable shop Bus Stop, run by designer Lee Bender.

Elisabeth Sladen wore this costume again in Doctor Who/EastEnders crossover *Dimensions in Time* (1993), shown in aid of charity Children in Need.

This childish-looking costume contrasts with what happens in *The Hand of Fear*, as Sarah is possessed by the wicked Eldrad and causes mayhem.

Destiny of the Daleks (1979): Costume designed by June Hudson
City of Death (1979): Costume designed by Doreen James
The Leisure Hive (1980): Costume designed by June Hudson

ROMANADVORATRELUNDAR ("ROMANA") II

Played by Lalla Ward

1979–1981

Lalla Ward hoped her costume might make wearing "these wretched things called school uniform" seem more attractive to children watching the show.

June Hudson originally sketched Edwardian women's bathing suits but thought them too cumbersome. Lalla wanted to look tomboyish, so they settled on a boy's Edwardian sailor suit.

At the start of *Destiny of the Daleks*, Romana wears an exact copy of the Doctor's own clothes. It was Lalla Ward's idea to have Romana dress like the Doctor.

In *The Leisure Hive* Romana is dressed to attend the public opening of the Brighton Pavillion in the 1850s — but the TARDIS never gets there.

"Goodness, I wish I'd never thought of it when I got that white scarf which hooked itself on to absolutely everything!"
— Lalla Ward

Dragonfire (1987): Costume designed by Richard Croft
Remembrance of the Daleks (1988): Costume designed by Ken Trew
The Curse of Fenric (1989): Costume designed by Ken Trew

DOROTHY ("ACE")

Played by Sophie Aldred
1987–1989

The Blue Peter badges on the jacket were Sophie Aldred's own, which she earned as a child.

The leggings and skirt were inspired by a trendy friend of Sophie's.

A photograph in fashion magazine *The Face* provided Ace's look.

The 1940s costume was short-sleeved and made of thin material because of a line in the script: "Is it this hot everywhere?"

Ace originally wore yellow and black striped tights but they caused strobing on the TV cameras!

Filming was beset with rain and snow, meaning the warm-weather outfit wasn't ideal!

Divided skirt for the penultimate scene in which Ace swims underwater

The Empty Child (2005): Costume designed by Lucinda Wright
Tooth and Claw (2006): Costume designed by Louise Page
The Idiot's Lantern (2006): Costume designed by Louise Page

ROSE TYLER

Played by Billie Piper

2005–2006, 2008, 2010, 2013

Rose's clothes in the 2005 series are "very bright and very bold," says Lucinda Wright, "very much like Rose the character."

Punk look because the Doctor meant to take her to see Ian Dury play at the Top Rank in Sheffield on 21 November 1979, but instead he lands them in Scotland a hundred years earlier

Helmet supplied by prop department, specially sprayed to match the dress

Dressed to see Elvis Presley perform 'Hound Dog' on *The Ed Sullivan Show* in New York in 1956, but they arrive in London in 1953

Doomsday and *The Runaway Bride* (2006): Costume designed by Louise Page
The Unicorn and the Wasp (2008): Costume designed by Louise Page
The Stolen Earth and *Journey's End* (2008): Costume designed by Louise Page

DONNA NOBLE

Played by Catherine Tate
2006, 2008–2010

In Russell T Davies' script for *The Stolen Earth*, there's no description of what Donna is wearing.

A complete version of this costume, worn by Catherine's stunt double, was sold at auction for £780.

Donna's first appearance in this striking dress, in the final scene of *Doomsday*, lasts just 13 seconds.

Our final sight of Donna is also in a wedding dress, when she marries Shaun Temple In *The End of Time: Part Two* (2010).

An original 1920s dress was hired specially for the episode *The Unicorn and the Wasp*, set in 1926.

Catherine Tate didn't like running in the satin court shoes, so often wore trainers!

Smith and Jones (2007): Costume designed by Louise Page
Gridlock (2007): Costume designed by Louise Page
Human Nature (2007): Costume designed by Louise Page

MARTHA JONES

Played by Freema Agyeman
2007, 2008, 2010

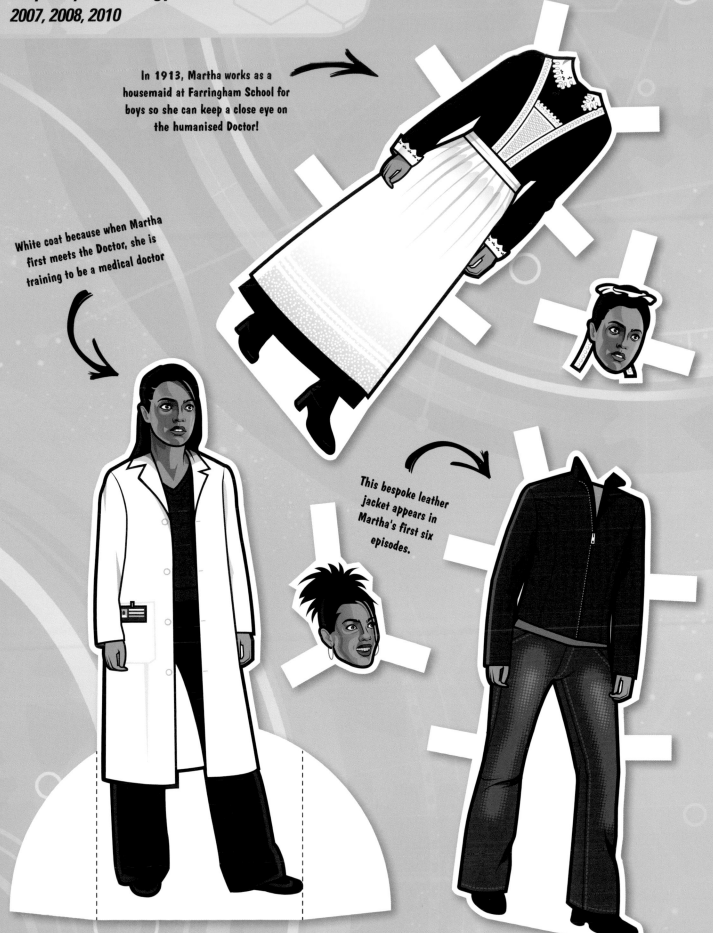

In 1913, Martha works as a housemaid at Farringham School for boys so she can keep a close eye on the humanised Doctor!

White coat because when Martha first meets the Doctor, she is training to be a medical doctor

This bespoke leather jacket appears in Martha's first six episodes.

The Pandorica Opens (2010): Costume designed by Ray Holman
Day of the Moon (2011): Costume designed by Barbara Kidd
The Angels Take Manhattan (2012): Costume designed by Howard Burden

RIVER SONG

Played by Alex Kingston

2008, 2010–2013, 2015

Dressed as private detective Melody Malone

The script describes "a slouch hat, as favoured by detectives in those kind of movies".

River changes into this outfit after falling from a New York skyscraper into the TARDIS swimming pool. Presumably it's from the TARDIS wardrobe.

Our first sight of River in her "ordinary" clothes. Before this, we've seen her in a spacesuit, a ballgown, army fatigues, a prison uniform, a black outfit for burglary and dressed as Cleopatra.

AMELIA "AMY" POND

Played by Karen Gillan
2010–2012, 2013

The script describes Amy donning a hat and doublet (a type of fitted jacket) to look like a "pirate queen".

Ray Holman discussed checked shirts and short skirts on the first day he met Karen — and it became Amy's signature look.

When the Doctor first meets grown-up Amy, she's not really a police officer but working as a kissogram.

"Short skirts show that Amy is confident and comfortable about her look," says Karen Gillan. "You have to have confidence to wear something like that!"

The Hungry Earth and *Cold Blood* (2010): Costume designed by Ray Holman
The Pandorica Opens (2010): Costume designed by Ray Holman
The Impossible Astronaut and *Day of the Moon* (2011): Costume designed by Barbara Kidd

RORY WILLIAMS

Played by Arthur Darvill
2010–2012

Rory later wore a similar outfit on his honeymoon and when rescuing Amy from Demon's Run.

Worn by Rory as an Auton duplicate in 102 AD

Shorts and T-shirt for visiting the baking hot desert in Utah, USA, but the episode was filmed in November, when it was actually very cold!

Practical clothes for adventuring

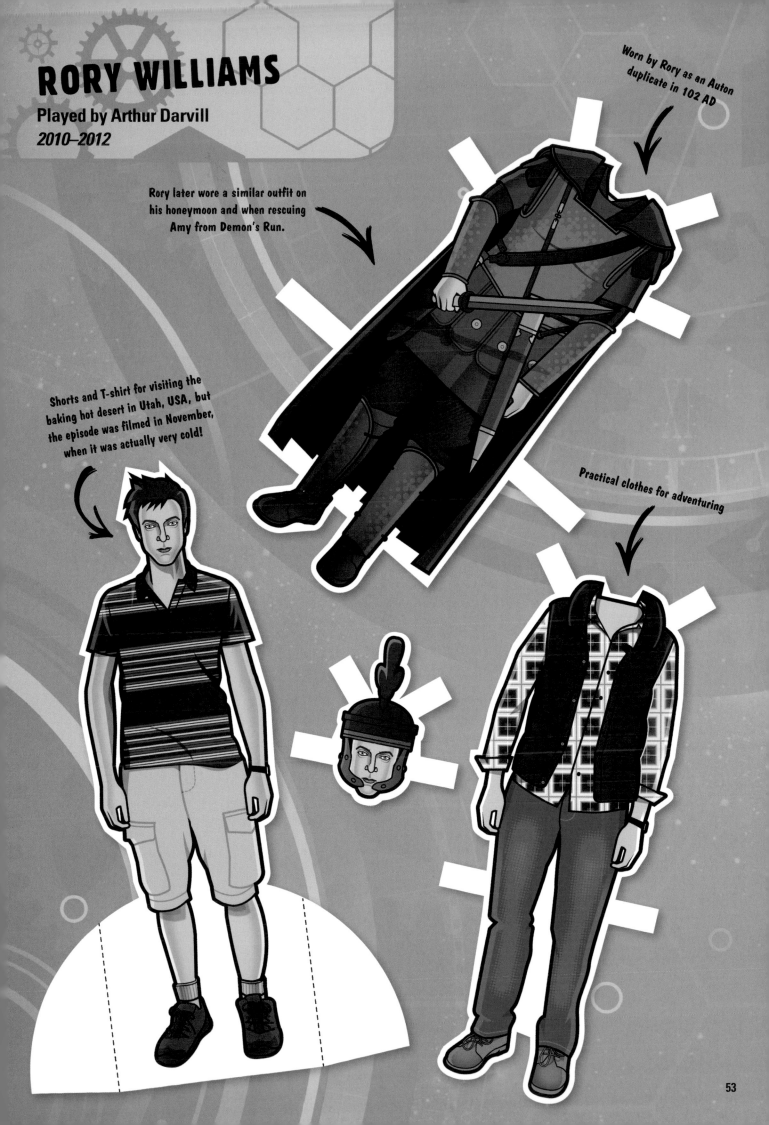

The Crimson Horror (2013): Costume designed by Howard Burden
Face the Raven (2015): Costume designed by Ray Holman
Hell Bent (2015): Costume designed by Ray Holman

CLARA OSWALD

Played by Jenna Coleman

2012–2015

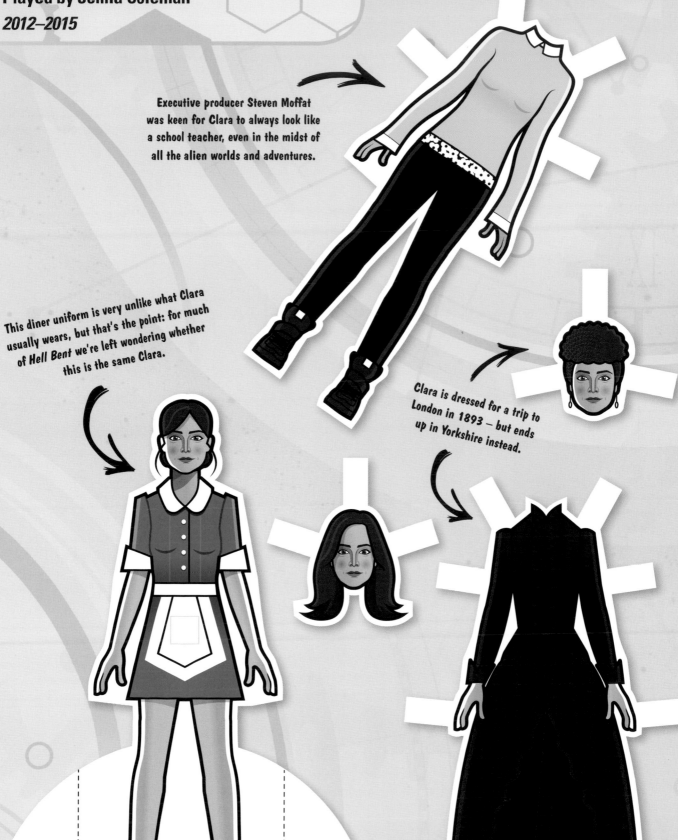

Executive producer Steven Moffat was keen for Clara to always look like a school teacher, even in the midst of all the alien worlds and adventures.

This diner uniform is very unlike what Clara usually wears, but that's the point: for much of *Hell Bent* we're left wondering whether this is the same Clara.

Clara is dressed for a trip to London in 1893 — but ends up in Yorkshire instead.

The Day of the Doctor (2013) Costume designed by Howard Burden
Death in Heaven (2014): Costume designed by Howard Burden
The Zygon Invasion (2015): Costume designed by Ray Holman

PETRONELLA OSGOOD

Played by Ingrid Oliver

2013–2015

Eleventh Doctor-style bow tie

Fifth and Sixth Doctor-style question-mark collar

Tenth Doctor-style trainers

Seventh Doctor-style tanktop, sourced from Lovarzi — the company who make officially licensed *Doctor Who* clothing for cosplayers!

"I love the cosplayers," says writer and executive producer Steven Moffat. "They're brilliant. So putting a cosplayer in the show was a sort of love letter to *Doctor Who* fandom."

Fourth Doctor-style scarf

Dark Water (2014): Costume designed by Howard Burden
Deep Breath (2014): Costume designed by Howard Burden

MISSY
Played by Michelle Gomez
2014–

Cameo brooch, made of dark star alloy and can cut through Dalek armour plating

Steven Moffat's description of Missy was "Mad Victorian nanny type".

In *Death in Heaven* (2014), Missy glides through the air with her umbrella up, and the influence on her look is clear: she's an evil Mary Poppins!

This dark costume, seen before Missy reveals who she is, offers a subtle clue to her identity, as the (male) Master often wore black costumes.

Friend from the Future (2016): Costume designed by Hayley Nebauer
The Pilot (2017): Costume designed by Hayley Nebauer
Smile (2017): Costume designed by Hayley Nebauer

BILL POTTS

Played by Pearl Mackie

2017–

Costume designer Hayley Nebauer wanted "to allow fans to be able to recreate this look in an affordable way".

Hayley stitched on the "wow" patch the night before shooting. There were originally more patches, but it was felt the jacket looked too much like Ace's.

T-shirt bought from a vintage shop in Soho, London, and inspired by artwork from Prince's 1984 album *Purple Rain*

Vintage printed silk headscarf supplied by the make-up department

In *Smile*, Bill goes to a warm planet with two suns, so the costume needed to be summery, youthful, colourful and fun.

"The jacket was good for the wintery scenes in the episode, while keeping the costume bright, fun and optimistic like the character."
— Hayley Nebauer

Yellow puffer jacket bought from a vintage shop

61